Writing: the team at *Normandie Junior* (Jean-Benoît Durand, Nathalie Lescaille, Estelle Vidard).
Acknowledgement to Marie du Mesnil-Adelée.
Illustrations: Emmanuel Cerisier, Sandrine Lemoult (mascot), Carlos da Cruz (map).
Art direction: Gaëlle Queval.
Layout: Aurélie Lachevre.
Translation: Claudine Vidard, Amanda Burris.
Cover: Emmanuel Cerisier.

2011, Éditions La Petite Boîte
www.lapetiteboite-edition.fr
87, boulevard des Belges - 76000 Rouen

ISBN 978-2-916538-42-6
Act 49-956 of July 16th, 1949 relating to publications for young people.

Printed in France by Lecerf Rouen Offset.
05-2011 - Copyright 1st published May 2007

D-Day

Chapter 1

Why did the war start?

The rising of Nazism

In 1930, there is something wrong with Germany. It is one of the countries which have been most badly struck by the world economical crisis. A lot of German people are out of work. The Nazi Party*, led by Adolf Hitler, comes into power in 1933. Hitler is a cunning man with a gift for talking to crowds. His politics is based on racism and hatred towards the communists and the Jews, all the people he thinks are responsible for the German defeat of 1918.

Hitler comes into power

Hitler takes full powers at the death of the German President in 1934. He is called the "Führer" (the "Guide"). The country becomes a dictatorship. All political parties except his are forbidden, so are trade unions. Those who oppose Hitler are arrested and sent to prison. The Jews are no longer allowed to work as civil servants, they are not allowed to marry non-Jewish Germans either. They lose their rights of vote too.

* Words in colour are explained on page 24.

DR-Mémorial de Caen.

In his book Mein Kampf, Hitler asserts that men are not equal. For him, the German people are part of a superior "species".

Pierre Vals/Mémorial de Caen.

In Paris, Occupation is obvious: signposts are written in German.

Getting ready for the war

Hitler aims at giving back his country the power it had in the past. He wants to create an empire. A lot of Germans approve of the idea. Hitler is also esteemed because he has managed to reduce unemployment. He initiates great projects, has roads built... In 1938, he annexes Austria and a part of Czechoslovakia where some Germans live. France and Great Britain do not interfere as their governments want to avoid war.

The outbreak of war

On September 1st, German soldiers invade Poland. This is too much for France and Great Britain and, two days later, both countries declare war on Germany. However, it doesn't stop the Germans, allied to the Russians, from taking hold of Poland and crushing it within three weeks.

What is called the "Phoney War"?

After September of 1939, The French anticipated the German invasion. The French soldiers built trenches behind the Maginot Line: a fort that protected the front and the country. But nothing happened until May of 1940... this is why this period is nicknamed "The Phoney War". The German army eventually invaded France through the Ardennes forest, which the French military had thought was impenetrable.

Chapter 2

The war becomes worldwide

The taking of Paris

Paris is taken on June 14th. Field-Marshal Pétain, head of government, signs the Armistice. It means the end of fights in France. They have lasted 15 days only. Then, in 1941, the U.S.A. joins the war. With Great Britain and the U.S.S.R. now opposed to Hitler, they fight Germany and the Axis countries, Italy and Japan. The war becomes worldwide.

From April to May 1940, German troops invade Norway, Denmark, the Netherlands and Belgium. Then, they go on with their offensive in France through the Ardennes.

Death camps

The Jews who have not fled abroad suffer more and more persecution. From 1942 on, the Nazis create a genocide. Hitler has the Jews arrested and imprisoned in concentration and extermination camps such as Auschwitz, in Poland. They die there, asphyxiated in gas-chambers.

Archives nationales américaines/Mémorial de Caen.

*The **deported** worked incredibly hard and were not nourished well in concentration camps. Many of them die of exhaustion.*

Learn+

Occupied France

From 1940 to 1942, France is divided into two parts. The North is held by the Germans. The South is ruled by the French government backing up the Germans.

The yellow star

From 1942 on, the Jews living in France are obliged to wear a yellow star made of material.

The Resistance gets organized

From summer 1940 on, the French rebel against the German occupants and their French collaborators. These resisters cut down phone lines and blow up trains... If they are caught, they are tortured and killed.

Fight must go on

On June 18th, 1940, General de Gaulle who has left France for England speaks to the French on the radio. He asks them to go on fighting.

Shortage of food

The Germans plunder France. Shops are nearly empty. Ration coupons are needed in order to get milk, flour or meat.

Towards victory

From the year 1942 on, the Axis Powers meet increasing resistance from the Allies in Africa, the Pacific and the U.S.S.R. In Italy, Dictator Mussolini is expelled and the Armistice is signed.

In France, the situation is complicated. The Germans have occupied the whole country since 1942. The Allies bomb factories, harbours and railway-stations in order to weaken the enemy. A lot of French people are killed and thousands of houses are destroyed.

Europe in November 1942

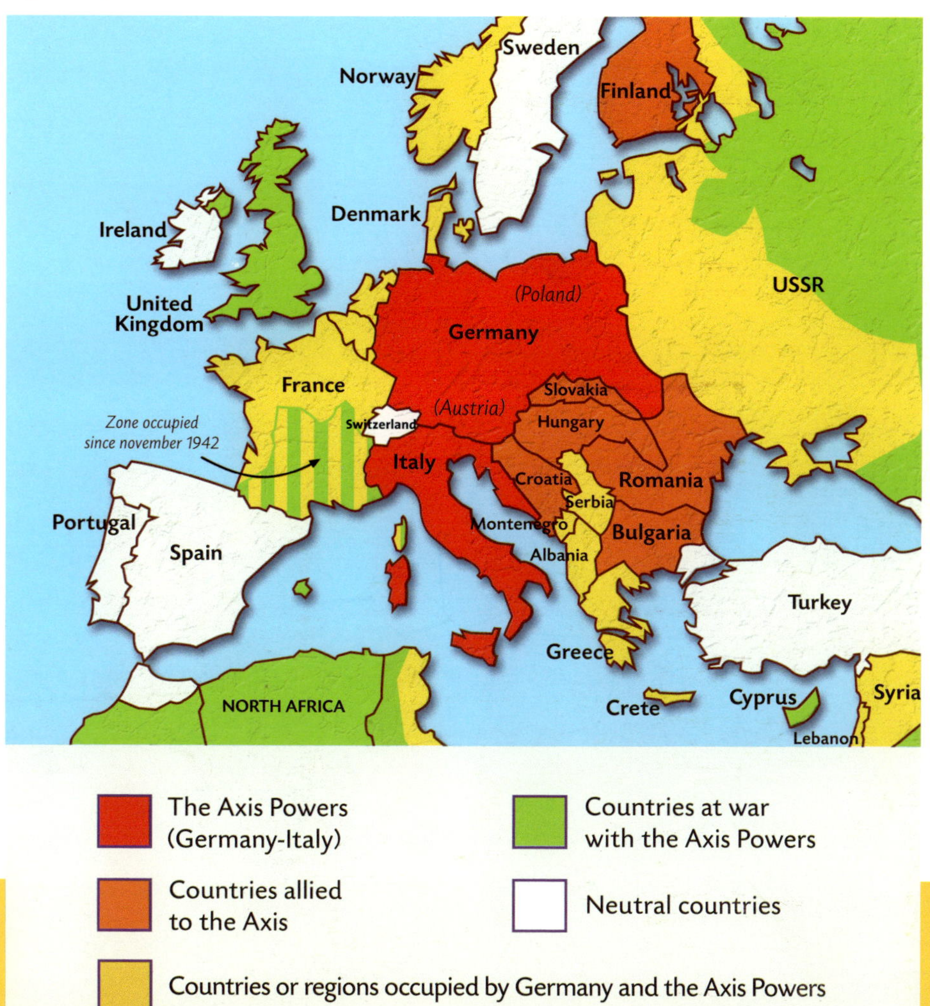

The Axis Powers (Germany-Italy)

Countries allied to the Axis

Countries or regions occupied by Germany and the Axis Powers

Countries at war with the Axis Powers

Neutral countries

Chapter 3

The landings in Normandy

0.00 Locating

British and American paratroopers are dropped on the Normandy coast, near Merville and Carentan. Their mission is to check that the landing areas the allied soldiers are expected to use are safe.

In order to liberate France, the Allies land on the Normandy beaches on D-Day. This operation, named Overlord, has been prepared in great secret. Here is the story of this incredible day.

0.15 am The first land-battles

British soldiers are set down by gliders near the bridges spanning the Orne and the Caen canal. The British have Bénouville and Ranville under control within a quarter of an hour.

The assault!

The soldiers land. The first assaults take place on two beaches called Utah and Omaha. The operation on Utah Beach is successful and the enemy surrenders but on Omaha Beach the Allies suffer severe casualties.

Risky parachuting

Thousands of planes and gliders drop 8,000 British and Canadian soldiers east of the landing zone and 13,000 Americans west. Many of them land in marshes and get drowned. The ones who have landed safely regroup.

A strategic point

Three companies of American Rangers climb the Pointe du Hoc between Utah and Omaha with hook ladders. They take possession of the top of the cliff where the Germans have posted their guns.

Armada in sight

7,000 ships escorted by planes are in sight of the beaches. The Germans are surprised: they thought the landing would take place in Pas-de-Calais. At dawn, the ships of the armada open fire to weaken the enemy.

A second wave

The British and Canadians storm three other beaches: Gold, Juno and Sword. At the same time, American reinforcements are being dispatched to Omaha Beach.

The troops are mostly made up of American, British and Canadian soldiers... But some French, Belgian and Polish men also take part in the landing.

1.30 pm Bayeux in sight

Artificial harbours are built in Arromanches-les-Bains and Saint-Laurent-sur-Mer to make the landing of men and their equipment easier. The Allies go on making their way towards Bayeux.

8.00 pm On the radio

General Eisenhower, Commander-in-Chief of the allied forces, breaks the news of the landing on the American radio. The first bombings on Caen start. Meanwhile, soldiers are gaining ground inland.

What is the "Battle of Normandy"?

On June 7th, 1944, the landing of the Allies is a success. But it is only the first step of the liberation of France! The next mission of the Allies is to free the rest of Normandy. From June 7th to August 21st 1944 they will fight without respite against the Germans. The towns of Bayeux, Cherbourg, Caen, Saint-Lô and Falaise will be gradually liberated. The Germans have lost the "Battle of Normandy" but it is responsible for the death of numerous soldiers on both sides.

Learn+

The landing beaches

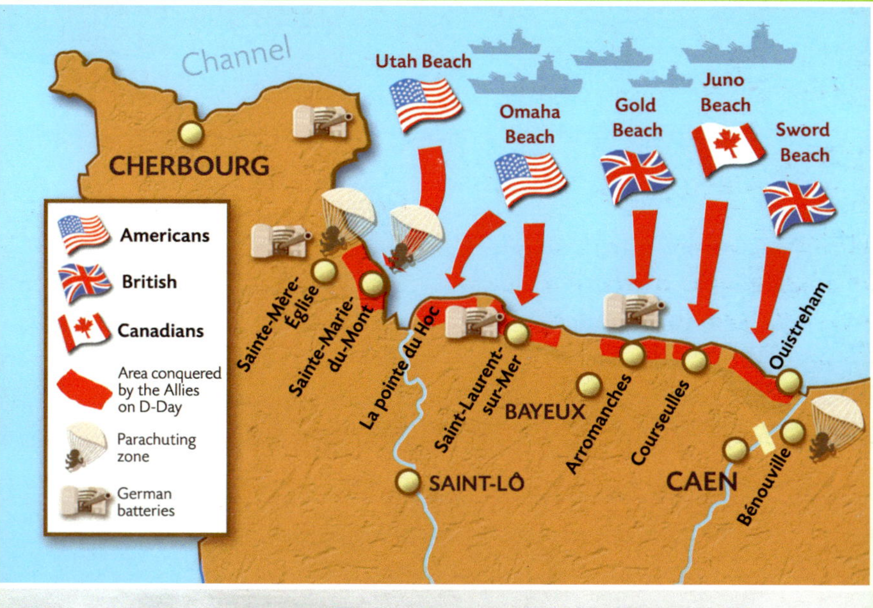

Archives nationales américaines/Mémorial de Caen.

Chapter 4

War is over!

Free at last!

The Allies liberate the territory little by little. Paris is liberated at the end of the "Battle of Normandy" on August 25th. The crowd waving French flags greet the allied soldiers with cheers. General de Gaulle is head of the new government of the French Republic. Accused of collaboration with the enemy, Pétain is sentenced to death. He is pardoned by De Gaulle and is eventually sent to prison where he dies a few years later.

After the landings, soldiers keep on fighting to liberate France. In order to help the allied soldiers gain ground, some towns are bombed. In Normandy, Le Havre, Caen and Saint-Lô are partly destroyed.

The end of the war

After France, Belgium and the Netherlands are gradually liberated. Germany is invaded. Hitler commits suicide on April 30th, 1945. On May 8th, Germany capitulates. In order to defeat Japan, the U.S.A. drops nuclear bombs on Hiroshima and Nagasaki. It is the end of World War II. Its consequences are awful: at least fifty million casualties!

Archives nationales du Canada.

The rebuilding of Normandy

Situated on the Channel coast, Le Havre is severely bombed. The destroyed area is rebuilt between 1945 and 1964 after the drawings of architect Auguste Perret. It is a fine example of post-war town-planning, mainly using concrete, the new material of the time. Nowadays, the town is a World Heritage site! It means it is a historical testimony which must be protected.

The town of Le Havre is rebuilt after the war. Concrete is widely used.

New Caen

The rebuilding of Caen lasts nearly 15 years. Very straight wide avenues are made to make traffic easier. Five-storey blocks of flats made of Caen stone are built along the streets.

A large university is created. In remembrance of the painful events of 1944, the town has erected a statue representing a phoenix. This mythological bird symbolizes the rising again from the ashes.

The Caen Memorial recounts the history from 1918 to modern times. It explains the breaking out of World War II and urges people to think about peace.

Games

D-Day

Quiz time

Have you read your book correctly? To test what you have learnt, answer these questions!

1 Which year does Hitler come into power?
A   In 1900.
B   In 1933.
C   In 1939.

2 What is the name of the party he leads?
A   The Nazi Party.
B   The Soviet Party.
C   The German Party.

3 What happens on September 1st, 1939?
A   Germany invades Poland.
B   France invades Germany.
C   Poland invades France.

4 When does the war become worldwide?
A   In 1939.
B   In 1940.
C   In 1941.

5 Who or what does Hitler attack first?
A   The Jews.
B   Women.
C   Animals.

6 Which countries are called the Allies?
A   Great Britain, the U.S.S.R., the U.S.A. and Canada.
B   France, Italy, Great Britain and Belgium.
C   Austria, Japan, China and Vietnam.

7 **Which symbol are the Jews obliged to sew on their clothes?**
A A green triangle.
B A pink rhomb.
C A yellow star.

8 **Where do the Allies land on D-Day?**
A In Normandy.
B In Alsace.
C In Provence.

9 **Which day is Paris liberated?**
A On June 7th, 1944.
B On July 15th, 1944.
C On August 25th, 1944.

10 **Which town in Normandy is a World Heritage site?**
A Rouen.
B Le Havre.
C Caen.

Answers: see page 24.

Around Caen and Bayeux

**To find out more about the World War II historical sites and D-Day, visit:
www.normandiememoire.com**

• **The Caen Memorial** recounts the history from 1918 to modern times. It tempts you to a great trip into history to understand World War II and the Cold War which followed. The museum also urges you to think about peace. Do not miss the temporary exhibitions either.
Esplanade Eisenhower. Tel. 02 31 06 06 45. www.memorial-caen.fr

• **The Battle of Normandy Memorial Museum** in Bayeux recalls the days that followed D-Day, from June 7th until August 29th, 1944. The museum has weapons, uniforms, materials and armor on display inside and outside.
*Boulevard Fabian-Ware.
Tel. 02 31 51 46 90.*

• In Bayeux, **the General de Gaulle Memorial** is a hotel where the General stayed on his way back from London. His personal items and some wartime radio equipment can be seen there.
*10, rue Bourbesneur.
Tel. 02 31 92 45 55.*

• In Saint-Martin-des-Besaces, **the Fighting in the Bocage Museum** tells the adventure of soldiers in the Vire bocage in stunning scenes.
*5, rue du 19-Mars-1962.
Tel. 02 31 67 52 78.*

• **The Battle of Tilly Museum** at Tilly-sur-Seulles retraces the combats hour by hour during the first three weeks following D-Day.
*Chapelle Notre-Dame-du-Val.
Tel. 06 07 59 46 02. www.museetilly.free.fr*

• Among the main sites of the Battle of Normandy, you have access to archived films and historical and tourist information simply by using the Mob E mobile phones. *www.normandiememoire.com*

Around Sword Beach

• In Bénouville, stop at **Gondrée Café**. It is the first house which was liberated on June 6th, 1944. Pegasus Memorial stands 200 metres further on. This museum tells about the first victory of the British force on the night of June 5th, 1944. Pegasus Bridge, at the heart of the battle, stands in the park.
Avenue du Major-Howard. Tel. 02 31 78 19 44.

• In Ouistreham, **the No.4 Commando Museum** is devoted to the landing of French and British soldiers.
4, place Alfred-Thomas.
Tel. 02 31 96 63 10.

• In Merville, **the Battery Museum** recounts the attack of British paratroopers against a fortified German position. It is set up in a bunker.
Place du 9ᵉ Bataillon. Tel. 02 31 91 47 53.

• In Ouistreham, **the Atlantic Wall Museum** is a huge blockhouse, an old German position. Visit the transmission room, the armoury and the soldiers' room.
14, avenue du 6-Juin. Tel. 02 31 97 28 69.

Around Juno Beach

• In Courseulles-sur-Mer, **the Juno Beach Centre** praises the part played by Canadians during the war. Follow the characters Madeleine and Peter along the exhibition. Juno Park is a history trail among the sand dunes.
Voie des Français-Libres.
Tel. 02 31 37 32 17. www.junobeach.org

Centre Juno Beach / G. Wait.

Near Gold Beach

• In Ver-sur-Mer, a section of **the America-Gold Beach Museum** is devoted to the landing of British soldiers on Gold Beach and the liberation of the first French town, Bayeux.
2, place Amiral-Byrd. Tel. 02 31 22 58 58.

• In Longues-sur-Mer, **the German Battery** is one of the few which have kept their guns.
5km east of Port-en-Bessin via D6. Tel. 02 31 21 46 87.

• In Arromanches-les-Bains, **the Landing Museum** explains with models the building of the artificial harbour by the Allies.
Place du 6-Juin. Tel. 02 31 22 34 31.

• In a circular hall, **Arromanches 360 Cinema** shows a film depicting the landing on nine large screens. A stunning journey to the heart of the action!
Chemin du Calvaire. Tel. 02 31 22 30 30. www.arromanches360.com

Near Omaha Beach

• In Saint-Laurent-sur-Mer, **the Omaha Beach Memorial Museum** displays a collection of army vehicles, weapons, uniforms and badges.
Rue de la Mer. Tel. 02 31 21 97 44. www.musee-memorial-omaha.com

• **The Omaha D-Day Museum** in Vierville-sur-Mer displays military supplies allowing visitors to understand the technological evolution during war and their consequences on daily life.
Route de Grandcamp-Maisy. Tel. 02 31 21 71 80.

• In Grandcamp-Maisy, **the Pointe du Hoc** is a battlefield which is still exactly as it was when the Rangers left it on June 8th, 1944. Be sure to visit the **Maisy Battery** as well!
Quai Crampon. Tel. 02 31 22 64 34.

Near Utah Beach

• At the **Azeville Battery**, walk along the 350 metre-long underground galleries and watch a film about the building of the Atlantic Wall.
Between Sainte-Mère-Église and Montebourg. Tel. 02 33 40 63 05.

• **Sainte-Mère-Église** village was made famous by the film "The Longest Day". American paratroopers took hold of it on D-Day at 4.30 am. One of them even landed on the church steeple! Near the church, the Airborne Museum is devoted to paratroopers. A plane, a glider, a jeep, some parachutes and figures in genuine wartime costumes can be seen there.
14, rue Eisenhower. Tel. 02 33 41 41 35.
www.airborne-museum.org

• In Quinéville, **the Memorial to Regained Freedom** tells about daily life during the war: food, travel, requisitioning, the part played by women and children...
18, avenue de la Plage. Tel. 02 33 95 95 95.
www.memorial-quineville.com

• In Sainte-Marie-du-Mont, **the Landing Museum** is set up in a blockhouse. You will find models and archives there.
Tel. 02 33 71 53 35.

• **The D-Day Paratrooper Historical Center** at Saint-Côme-du-Mont recounts the violent combats that were fought in this region by the American paratroopers against the Germans.
2, village de l'Amont. Tel. 02 33 42 00 42.

• In Saint-Marcouf-de-l'Isle, at the **Crisbecq Battery Museum**, visit the converted bunkers, the soldiers' room and the infirmary and enjoy live historical scenes!
Route des Manoirs. Tel. 06 68 41 09 04.
www.batterie-marcouf.com

Near Avranches

• **The Mont-Ormel Memorial** recalls the last fights of the Battle of Normandy.
Tel. 02 33 67 38 61.

• In Val-Saint-Père, **the World War II Museum** and its figures in uniforms recount the "Avranches fights" which were the starting point to the great offensive of the Allies towards Paris.
Le Moulinet. Tel. 02 33 68 35 83.

In Cherbourg

• **The Fort du Roule Liberation Museum** tells the epic story of the harbour during the Liberation thanks to models, films and scenes showing daily life, particularly that of children.
Tel. 02 33 20 14 12.

In Orne

• In Alençon, **the Leclerc Museum** tells about Marschal Leclerc's epic role and the story of the liberation of Alençon.
33, rue du Pont-Neuf. Tel. 02 33 26 27 26.

• In L'Aigle, **the June 1944 Museum** recounts the Battle of Normandy with waxwork figures and the voices of Churchill and De Gaulle...
Place Fulbert-de-Beina. Tel. 02 33 84 16 16.

In Seine-Maritime

• In Ardouval, on **Val-Hygot site**, discover a launching ramp for V1 flying bombs.
On the edge of Eawy Forest. Tel. 02 33 83 90 66.

• In Forges-les-Eaux, **the Resistance and Deportation Museum** displays weapons, costumes, badges, posters and leaflets.
Rue du Maréchal-Leclerc. Tel. 02 35 90 64 07.

Dictionary

The Allies: the countries which fought against the Germans during the war: Great Britain, the U.S.S.R., the U.S.A. and Canada.

Annex: absorb a territory into a country.

Armada: a fleet of ships.

Armistice: an agreement to stop war.

Deportee: a person sent to a concentration camp.

Genocide: systematic killing of a whole people.

Mythological: related to myths and legends.

Nazi Party: led by Hitler, it was from 1920 on his means of getting power. A single party government.

Town-planning: the rebuilding or improving of a town.

U.S.S.R.: former state located in Europe and Asia.

Quiz answers

Page 18: 1B; 2A; 3A; 4C; 5A; 6A; 7C; 8A; 9C; 10B.

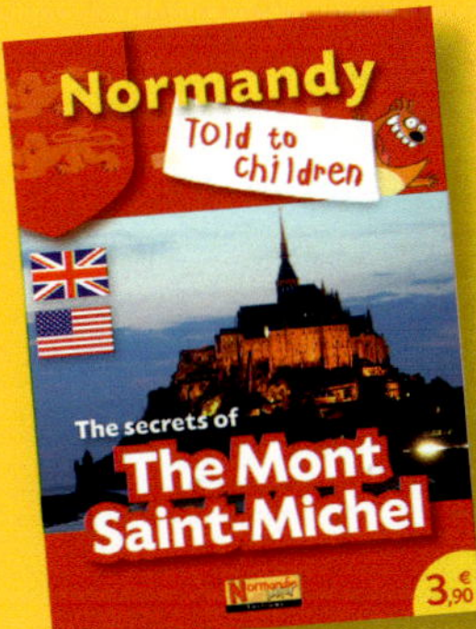

🇬🇧 HAPPY FAMILIES

Discover all our books on: www.lapetiteboite-edition.fr